VEII AND OTHER POEMS

ALSO BY ROBERT WELLS FROM CARCANET

*Collected Poems and Translations*
*The Day and Other Poems*
*Lusus*
*Selected Poems*
*The Winter's Task*

TRANSLATIONS
Virgil, *The Georgics*
Theocritus, *The Idylls*

# VEII AND OTHER POEMS

*Robert Wells*

CARCANET POETRY

First published in Great Britain in 2021 by
Carcanet
Alliance House, 30 Cross Street
Manchester, M2 7AQ
www.carcanet.co.uk

A CIP catalogue record for this book is
available from the British Library.

ISBN 978 1 80017 128 2

Book design by Andrew Latimer
Printed in Great Britain by SRP Ltd, Exeter, Devon

The publisher acknowledges financial
assistance from Arts Council England.

# CONTENTS

# 3

*For my granddaughter*
FLORA

VEII AND OTHER POEMS

# 1

## A LAST LOOK

You are already leaving, the hills are closed
And this the goodbye after the last goodbye,

A last look back at the sprawling riverbed
Where what you had looked for stepped clear into view

– There that midday, at pause among the willows,
Embodied shade, drawn out of indistinctness

To form and colour, solidly visible,
Confirmed by air and water in its daydream.

# THE COIN CABINET

*(five trays)*

## 1

Two calves' heads face to face, between them a tree.
A youth holding in a horse stung by a bee.
A parsley leaf. A corn-ear. A bunch of grapes.
An Amazon. A nymph whom a satyr rapes.
An opening rose. A swan flourishing its wings.
A prow. A tripod. A lyre with seven strings.
A crab, its pincers poised to repel attack.
A stag crouched with a clawing lion on its back.
A charioteer and team as they win the race
And take the prize. A spring, Arethusa's face
Freshly shaped in the water as it wells up.
Horse-tailed Silenos seated, tilting a cup.

## 2

A dolphin-rider above a curling sea.
A girl, half-stripped, in the branches of a tree,
Straddled by a bird, a bullock's head below.
Wrestlers grappling. An archer stringing a bow.
A double axe-head. A wheel. A vase. A lamp.
Thetis veiled, reclining on a hippocamp.
Herakles with the lion in his stranglehold,
Lovingly locked. A horned griffin guarding gold.
A turtle with spread flippers and studded shell
Paddling onward, aslant in the glassy swell.
Pan fagged with hunting, leant on a crag to rest
And turning to catch the breeze across his chest.

## 3

A gathered apple. Date-clusters on a palm.
Athena at war, her shield on her raised arm,
Spear poised. A brandished trident. A thunderbolt.
A cow scratching its muzzle. A prancing colt.
A ram. A tortoise. A bounding hare. A dove.
The sun-god's car, an eagle planing above.
A scarab-beetle. Two writhing snakes. A frog,
Softly defenceless. Unleashed, a hunting-dog
Seizing a fawn by the throat. Three seals at play.
A perched owl staring beside an olive-spray.
A feathered daimon. Gorgon baring her teeth.
A strutting cock. A pomegranate. A wreath.


## 4

A sea-eagle plucking its prey from the waves.
The head of a Maenad, wild-haired as she raves.
A Hydra. A Chimaera. A winged boar.
A soaring Pegasos. A squat Minotaur.
A Sphinx half-sitting, her slenderly curled haunch
A-quiver. Phoibos waving a laurel branch.
Hyakinthos kneeling, in his hand a flower.
Four horses at the gallop: one surge of power;
A snapped rein trailing, the turning-column down.
An old man with puckered face and balding crown.
Young Hermes gazing beneath his hat's broad brim
At the new shades that gather to follow him.

## 5

Two girls who carefully lift an amphora.
A discus-whirling boy. A crescent and star.
The head of Zeus, thick-bearded, intently calm.
Poseidon, a wave-worn cloak across his arm.
A sea-perch raising its spiky length of fin.
A close-fleshed tunny, tight in its oval skin,
Hauled from the water. Eight-armed, a cuttle-fish.
A priestess by her altar, holding a dish.
A tensile vine. Dionysos, grave and slack,
Stretching comfortably on a donkey's back.
Demeter crowned with harvest, veil loosely furled
To greet her daughter, back from the underworld.

## IONIAN

*O estuaries, anchorages*

          that bay
where the fresh meeting the salt water
ran cold above it,
and the swimmer there
churning the levels together
started with his movement
– by some chemistry –
a precipitate,
clouding about his limbs.

*O harbours, hinterlands*

          a broken
sarcophagus on the foreshore;
a line of arches, weatherworn,
striding with vain purpose
into the wood
– too easily whetted
a taste for elegy,
the greeds and cruelties
long gone elsewhere.

*O ragged coasts, rough capes*

          the boat riding
offshore where no beach opened
– heave of water
against the abrupt stone,
a pine grove where cicadas
scratched their song so loud

by hot mid-morning
that the sound came
distinct across the surge.

    *O fellow-travelling creatures*

        dolphins
within the prow's torn backwash
rising alongside,
embodiments of the wave
– suddenly outside it
and ahead in varied play,
the propulsion without visible cause;
so, stationary-seeming
as if stamped in silver.

    *O evidences of passage*

        ruts in rock,
a coin, a figurine,
potsherd litter, an amulet
pulled from riverbank gravel
– less these leavings
than the journey retrieved and known,
sea true to its old epithets,
day measured by the sun
lifting and sinking.

## LOGGERHEAD

Type of a courage to which the heart, intent
On its own journey, answers:
                              the sea-turtle,
Unwieldy solitary, tilted aslant,
Ferrying itself along through the green swell.

## LYCIAN SKETCHES

### 1

Stone tombs like hold-alls
abandoned on a station platform,

in the shade an old sailor
come back to his own village;

the rock-ridge necropolis arid
above a red-soiled valley

where corn in circles
is being threshed and winnowed.

### 2

Marshbound waters, silted havens,
sites quick with traffic
turned to enclaves of fever:

O pastoral by default!

– a quayside granary, its rugged façade
and foursquare walls
become a picturesque item,
glimpsed unreachably
across a vista of reeds.

## THE GARDEN

*i.m. Brenda Dowson*

What remains of those forays
when, girlish as ever,
you'd set off in your light
blue sunhat, with brisk light tread –
gloves, trowel, secateurs
and cigarettes in hand,
as ever exclaiming
at how late you'd left it,

*O my godfathers*
– sure-footed on the mule-track
despite your seventy,
your eighty years… to the same
vacant stretch of meadow,
your garden? It never took shape!
A few untended roses
and straggling oleanders

still make a doubtful show
between the olives and vines,
with – here and there – the flourish
of some staunch denizen
returning, spring by spring,
to the nook you found for it
among scabius and chicory
one bygone afternoon.

What became of that effort,
those hours, that fantasy
which drew you into its trance,
conjuring time and to spare
for the piecemeal task
while you lived for the day
imagined, imaginary
when all would coalesce?

How was it I didn't see
that those rapt intervals
enacted a kind of dare:
coolly, continuously,
you were flouting an opponent,
who must surely be around,
impalpable stalker,
somewhere just out of range?

Here, under long grass,
the little travertine plaque
marks with initials and dates
where your expatriate ashes
were emptied illegally out,
the urn flown home, its customs
paperwork in order –
containing household cinders:

your wish, our subterfuge!
No cemetery should have you,
least of all the dapper
precinct in silhouette
(if ever from your side
of the valley you glanced across)
on the slope above the village,
squared off with cypresses.

For death you had no time.
You carried yourself proudly
as if to hold it away
by the sheer dismissive force
of your prejudice, that stare
practised in youth to guard
a beauty which turned heads,
those put-downs you reserved

for some awkward hanger-on
sent packing: 'not exactly
a ball of fire', or 'actually
I feel sorry for him'. So
you'd bend to your transplanted
orchids, your slips and seedlings
intently, with much to do,
disdaining interruption.

Death had to come in secret
(you would have refused to allow,
even had you suspected it,
that you had been accosted):
a tick, a horse-fly bite,
some trivial annoyance
to be brushed off or ignored;
the sequelae unremarked

through blankly ensuing days
of misidentified fever,
which you sought to scare away
with the rattle of the pill-box;
no inkling till, ten minutes
before the end, a felt
shift, and the words you left
till last, 'I think I'm dying'.

How vulnerably defiant
you were out on that open
hillside, or later in the high-walled
derelict *vasca* behind
the mill, your 'watergarden'
(the name was almost enough):
your last least-realized dream,
the one most real to you.

Where the stream fans idly
through willowherb and briar
– your stepping-stones displaced
under gravel or grassy mud –
no trace now of the cherished
vision which kept you busy,
no remnant visible
of all your interventions,

except... except for this clump
of dark bamboos, their smoky
stems asway, their fibrous
leaves uneasily sighing
as they brush against one another
in graceful discontent
– a thriving rarity
fetched here and planted by you.

Your emblem, your self unselved! –
as if, evasive still
even in the desperate moment,
you had, as your one recourse
to baffle the pursuit,
abruptly shed your body
and fled into the bamboo
and transformed were still here.

## WINTER CLASSROOM, L'AQUILA

My truant pupils
come in, brown from skiing,
matter-of-factly unapologetic
(the low sky sullen again
after dry fine days).

They bring an absence with them
neither room nor hour
nor my contrived insistences
dispel.
       Wide-eyed, spaced-out,
for them first things are happening
and still to happen
on the drifted blankness of the slopes,

the track they leave there only incidentally
their own, a gliding into distance,
body continuous
with sun and snow.

## ANTONELLO

The basketball court is overgrown with grass.
Only in my mind
The boy who used to play there exists still
And repeats his gesture of greeting as I go by.

## ACROSS DISTANCE

Relations formal, proper, of the slightest,
So that they may be hardly said to exist,
Yet within the formality go as deep
As the foundations of self;
                                            a hand half-raised
To greet, and in that gesture across distance
All of fellow-feeling, all of connection –

Not that two recognise each other merely,
Something more: a sign that within each other
The faculty exists of recognition.

## A HOMECOMING

*(Scene: a village piazza in the Sabine hills, circa 1965.)*

What do you think of your new son,
Mother, when he comes back from Rome?

He seems quite another one
When, a brief truant, he comes home.

The bus spills out the evening post
And people back for the holiday,

And no one else here's looking lost
Or changed from when they went away.

What did he go to Rome for, then?
The lamp shines on his roughening cheek.

Why is he laughing with the men
Though to you he hardly dares to speak?

What has he spent his money on?
He brings no token for his whims

Nor toy that cost him. Look at your son.
He moves more easily in his limbs.

IN THE ABRUZZI

The incident discovers its meaning now –
At least, such sense as can be attributed
After forty years…

                    A sunlit city square,
Low houses shuttered against the afternoon,
A fountain trickling into its bowl, a church,
Locked, the stone frontage darkly corrugated,
Rough walls and basalt pavement giving back heat.

On the further side, parked in a strip of shade,
Not seen at first, a bus – a blue *corriera*
Of the always-superannuated kind
That serves the mountain villages, and tumbles
The postbag out together with passengers;
Picks up, sets down at unnamed halts and by-ways,
Its horn listened out for along hairpin roads.

The driver not yet arrived, the little crowd
It brought to town this morning gathers by it –
Country people with their bundles and baskets,
Pleased to linger and gossip, their errands done.

At the near corner stands a kiosk, displaying
Newspapers, lottery tickets, cigarettes,
Biscuits and sweets, and a box or two of fruit.
Some of the passengers press round the counter,
Reaching over each other excitedly
To make last-minute purchases. I stop too
For some small item.

                    Shut in my own concerns,
I hardly notice the stir in front of me
Until it takes a more particular form:
A thickset elderly man in a black hat,
Dark coat and tieless shirt, buttoned at the neck –
A *contadino's* garb – begins to bargain
For a large bunch of bananas, which (a sum
Settled upon after much fine deployment
Of rhetoric) he clumsily endeavors
(Clutching a canvas umbrella tight beneath
One elbow) to manoeuvre into his bag,
Its zip catching, its imitation leather
Stiff and cracked.
                    Suddenly, exuberantly,
He swings about to face me (having put down
The bananas on the counter) and holds out
The empty bag by the handles: 'Tienilo,
Che sei giovane!' He looks me up and down –
A short pause – fixes his eyes on mine, and adds
In a voice both mocking and tenderly meant,
The words clear and deliberate as his stare,
'Figlio del biondo Apollo, fratello
Delle Muse! '
                    Then, as if rallying me
At my surprise and somehow disappointed
In his challenge, 'Ma sei educato, eh?'

Inwardly delighted, inwardly reproached,
I have no come-back. I hold the bag as asked
While he transfers the bananas; taking it,
He thanks me curtly, turns, strolls off to the bus –
Now opened by the driver – and climbs aboard,
Disappearing at once among the others.

Nonplussed, I make my purchase, stand there and watch
As the rackety vehicle pulls slowly
Round the fountain-basin and out of the square,
Carrying him, unplaceable as he seems,
Seer or showman, back to where he came from.

> Sons of blonde Apollo, the Muses' brother,
> Are two-a-penny. What makes the difference
> Is how each lives up to the salutation
> In the long sequel.
>                     As in the first instant,
> Touched by the occasion, unequal to it?

Many times I have imagined that village,
The bus finding its way by an unknown road
To a lost canton, happily off the map,
Where an old rite and shrine remain undamaged
Perhaps, as the perennial fable recounts;
Where the angst and inhibition clouding youth,
Blinding it to its luck, are lifted away,
The hidden godhead recognized and challenged.

If grove and glade are archaic words to him
The archaism belongs to early rising,
The hour of sleep forgone, a shadow clinging
To the active body, slowing thoughts and speech
To the steep path in twilight – caught as he is
Drowsily in the wonder of his waking:
Under the grey crest of the 'Campanile',
One with the others, step by step, he follows
Up to the hills, the wooded pasture, thinking
And speaking no faster than he treads, ready
For the day as daylight is, no readier –
As gradually it comes, is all around
Equal and full and clear, but shadow-haunted
As the young body is that matches morning.

\*

Scarcely to be known again, that first freshness
Except as morning surprises him sometimes
Bringing it back, or a reminiscence back.
Where are the welcome, the response, the promise?
The place remains, is at a thought recovered
Thin as it may be, shadow without body.
He is at the spring or in the bramble-glade
Or charcoal-burners' abandoned grove, or treads
Impalpably some stretch of familiar path
Or lingers to pull dew-chilled figs from the tree
In the meadow by the road, thirsty once more –
The cattle numbered and watered, and the day
Almost over, his intimation tells him,
The sun having just now reached the valley-floor.

# 2

## UNFINISHED LINES

From an old draft:

> 'At midday he lit the fire
> Where the high ridge was littered with his toil,
> And braided smoke like a blue stalagmite
> Rose, as the wind moved, through the green and brown,
> Became a column of oily fluent heat
> Until fumes leapt before the battening flame,
> As seasons hoarded in the disparate waste
> Broke down to ash and melted into air.
>
> All the afternoon the fire was burning,
> The sea very brimmed and vigorous below,
> Curded with white, very near. Often the wind
> Brought drifting rains amid the caves of air
> To generate a rainbow, curved complete
> From sea to sea on either side the ridge,
> And to the left a promontory set
> Its dark forepaw upon the glittering world.
>
> Cleared now all that was cut. Crouching at dusk
> He watched the colours the fire burned among,
> And felt at last by labour purified
> Of the weariness that slackened through his limbs,
> Made pitilessly new.
>                           But more and more
> His eyes dwelt heavily where they fell, his limbs
> Forgot their power. The various light was failing
> From clouds and sea – so that he came to himself
>
> Shivering, to learn how soon found wanting, how…'

How to finish?
              I rearrange some words,
See at once what lines must go, what phrases
Come stamped by fact. But as for a conclusion,
That belongs elsewhere, if in any lines
Which I could write even now; would have to wait
For years, for decades, while I broke my way
Out of the crystal prison enclosing him.

## FROM AN OLD NOTEBOOK

*'Hand touches hand...'*

Hand touches hand. It would not close on doubt.
A branch but touches earth, it strikes a root –

But touches branch, and welds the sticky bark.
Hope touches hope, or bleaches in the dark.


*Ash*

Cancelled finally even of flame
White-soft circle cold as the morning –

Adhering to a ghostly structure
A balance that breaks at tread or touch


*Dusk*

He watches how an oak-tree frets
The moonrise, how the star that sets

At the other limit of his view
Kindles within its depth of blue.

## THE FALL OF WINSTON
*an Exmoor fable*


He was the household favourite,
a handsome border collie,
two years old (his pedigree
immaculate), with a glossy
coat, its cream-and-tan
luxuriantly flouncing
as he pranced and leapt among us,
or streaming out as he raced;

the paragon at once
of beauty and good-nature,
petted and friendly, yet
preserving a seductive
aloofness. Who could fail
to be flattered by attentions
from such a creature, himself
the centre of attention?

A quarter trained perhaps
(the rest, so ran the hopeful
refrain, would come in time),
he sat beside his master
in the Land Rover, a companion,
the dog from the great house,
and would spring out with a flourish,
momentarily at heel,

when, in the lambing season,
his master toured the farms
and stayed to share the labour.
So, when the fields were walked
last thing in the evening
to ensure that the young lambs
were with their dams, the doubles
together, properly paired,

Winston had only to appear
in a field-corner, by the gate,
like a transfigured fox,
to make the ewes look up
alarmed and, suddenly reminded,
look about them for their young.
The pairing-off at dusk
went smoothly. He was good for that.

But with other tasks, wherever
steadiness or accurate
obedience were called for,
he was something of a joke.
The tenants and the farm-hands
looked on, and did not smile,
fearing, where they saw a weakness,
that the moor might find it out.

His master would send Winston
to run with the working dogs;
it seemed he couldn't or wouldn't
learn from them. They knew
to a T what was required,
what was permitted. Living
by rule in little packs,
competing among themselves,

they ignored him, as a nuisance
sometimes in their way.
Fawning, observant, instantly
reactive, neither beautiful
nor ugly, they looked for commands
where he would look for favours
– an exception would at least
be made for any failure.

Winston had his kennel
at the back of the great house
by the kitchen door (and dined there
on choicest scraps). At night
he was shut out – no need
to chain him. Where would he go,
secluded as the house was
under steep wood-hung coombs?

So too by day, off duty,
he had the run of the garden,
its terraced lawns, its rosebeds,
on a shelf above sheer cliffs.
The farms were a mile away
or further, up on the moor,
over the brow of the seaward
escarpment, looking inland.

As he circuited the garden
Winston, briskly high-stepping,
had worn a path in the lawn.
A clear line athwart the even
expanse and encompassing
the house, it surely signalled
that he belonged, had his part
– superfluous as that might be –

in the routine of the place.
It was noted with affection
from the dining-room, the parlour,
from the library bay-window:
there it was, Winston's track,
and there he was, too, rounding
a corner, combed by the breeze,
on his swift absorbed patrol.

Word came from the farms one day:
a dog had been worrying sheep
in the top fields. Pregnant ewes
had been found bloodied and harried
on several mornings. A stray dog
(our thoughts fixed angrily
on the outcast interloper).
A watch would be kept. Word came

that the dog resembled Winston,
that it was Winston. The truth
broke by degrees, eked out
with tact, on successive days…
Hill-farmers' eyes don't make
mistakes, not in such matters:
Winston's night-wandering
stood confirmed. As for the proof

– though it only served to clinch·
the fact already known –
his mouth was opened, his teeth
examined. There, at the back,
around the base of his molars,
lay twisted in, tell-tale,
a deposit of encrusting
grey-white strands of fleece.

Winston was a dead dog
from that moment. Nothing was said.
I, deaf to the unspoken,
supposed he would be confined
merely – as he was that night.
A way out would be devised
no doubt, some practical
adjustment made… Next morning,

neither sadly nor angrily
– it was all that remained to do,
a last formality –
his master unchained Winston
and drove him to the vet
(the favourite's privilege
to be 'put down' – a farm-dog
would have been shot out of hand).

There could be no goodbyes
of course – an obscenity
to allow him back among us.
The moor held, unforgiving,
to its tried and rigid law:
such a dog is incorrigible,
cannot be trusted, the taste
once got is never forgotten…

Proscription without appeal!
I learnt of it afterwards,
his master's quiet aside
that evening in the kitchen,
the table cleared: Winston
in the Roman phrase, 'had lived'.
That was all. And no one
mentioned him again.

Years later, revisiting
the house, I willed myself
to try his name, and asked
(my question half-concealed
amid other reminiscence)
what they, his master's son
– a child then – and his master
recalled of the incident.

No response. For his master
the name, the dog, the event
had gone clean out of mind.
The son could just remember
that there had been such a dog
but nothing of what happened.
For me alone then – unless
he figures, as a caution,

in a farm-hand's anecdote –
he remains a presence still.
Whenever 'cruel necessity'
is invoked, or a 'criminal'
obsession is brought to light,
or event throws into relief
our conditional affections,
Winston bounds into view

with that lordly vitality
which could not plead for him
– as if he had just returned
through coombs seaming the hills
from a savage secret foray,
having found his long way up,
pricked on by unaccommodated
instinct, to the dark top fields.

## EXMOOR FEBRUARY

**1**

An early lambing:
life after slippery life
hauled into cold air.

**2**

In the yard-corner
a heap of carcasses, cleared
weekly by the Hunt.

**3**

Birth and death crowding
into the days: far frontiers
nearer, more exact.

**4**

A world's width enclosed
by fields named and known: Breakneck,
Middlemead, the Plat.

BY THE LOIRE

**1**

Grey heron –
its shadow in the water
more visible than itself.

**2**

A kingfisher
– or a torn scrap
of turquoise litter
snagged on a branch?

**3**

Ragged phoenix –
the cormorant, wings held open,
on its stone-island.

**4**

On grey water
         hardly visible
the gull floats –
         a buoyant shadow.

## KINGFISHER

seen again,
        known
by the glint, momentary it may be,
a metallic flash
          lit from within

or steady as the bird perches,

the light it gives off
larger than itself

## OUTSIDE

opening the door
I didn't know they were there

a noise of deer hooves

as they gathered themselves
away into the dark
a rush
       then silence

## TIME OUT

He wakes each morning
blurred by an energy
without aim or concentration

– the soft wishes
of a life become all wish.

His thoughts are of pools, sun-shafts,
dew-wet glades.

*

A plank-bridge above a stream,
the grain of the wood
worn clear by weather;
stopped there

he watches, not the water's flow
but how the light
vibrates along it

in a ceaseless dazzling wave.

## GROUP WITH LAPTOP

Like Poussin's shepherds confronted by the stone
Sarcophagus with its graven apophthegm
(Propped there discreetly, a skull stares back at them;
The river-god tilts his urn; their girl looks on
Breast bared, her loose drape gathered about her thigh;
An elegiac glint touches leaves and clouds –
While the foremost of them leans to test the words
With unbelieving finger and startled eye):

These also, in the energy of their prime
Surprised and challenged, taking their turn in time
As if no others had lived and died, now press
Forward raptly, shepherds as they might have been,
To spell out the message printed on the screen:
'I too was a receiver of consciousness'.

'WITH LIVELY STEP...'

With lively step
Or plodding resignation
I follow the track –
To the one destination.

What else remains to do,
Or what more to say?
Everyman, young or old,
Is on his way.

## THE SMILE

What I believe in is that open face.
Where that clear smile is to be found I go
Gratefully, as to a spring:
                        its pulsing flow
In some deserted and long-looked-for place.

## THE ALFRED JEWEL

Beast-mouth, enamelled face and golden fret:
In that fine pattern our attentions met.

I keep it from the years, our one shared day:
The little space where feeling was in play.

## QUESTION IN AGE

The things that happened, the material,
    The fit words that were there to find,
That had the solidity of true recall
And vivid sense, must they be left behind,

The sense and the solidity foregone –
    Mere shadow-memories in their place,
Eidola that words have no purchase on
But pass through, as in an underworld embrace?

## OLD POET

Gripped by the need, but not the impulse, to make
A shape from the shadows on that ghostly screen,

He stares across the expanse of Limbo Lake –
No depth, no surface, a flicker in between.

## SOTTO VOCE

*On a Translation of Virgil*

Augustus boasted he had been able
To find Rome brick and leave it marble.

Our Scholar now reverses the trick,
He finds Rome marble and leaves it brick.

\*

Our Scholar might well maintain
That brick, though a somewhat plain
Resource for projects imperial,
Makes an excellent building material.

*Belief*

This brave Professor would replace God with the thrill
Of contemplating a cabbage leaf's wrinkled frill.

*Poundian*

If you should visit 'the city of Dioce
Whose terraces' we're told 'are the colour of stars',
Take a trip to its suburb and be sure to see
The concentration camp there and the cattle cars.

*Collected Poems*

We learn, on page six hundred (as we pass
The halfway mark), that 'excellence is sparse'.

# 3

## AT KIRTLINGTON

I came here to search for fossils.
                                       Even and odd,
Matching lamellibranch, beaked brachiopod,
Slipped from the limestone shelf where they lay packed
At the tap of my hammer – name and fact
Declaring themselves frankly in my open palm,
Newly discovered shapes.
                                 The quarry, calm
As an empty amphitheatre, lay around
Wide-floored, vast in its space and air: a ground
Where I first sensed how it might be to accept
What, undeclared, must stay mere secret kept
For its own sake, locked in a brittle shelf –

So found I was less a stranger to myself.

## NEAR CHARNIZAY

The flint scraper loose on a white claybank
At the wood's edge, as if set there or mislaid
A moment since and waiting to be found,
The chipped blade crisply arching itself:

A shaped object chanced on, held, examined
As if for some proof or promise - but of what?

Not far off, the cave in an escarpment
Might have been just vacated. At its foot
A spring rises fresh as ever – water low-voiced
(I stoop to hear) putting its ancient question.

## THIS COIN

This coin, a little bronze of Rhegium,
Apollo's patinated head, crisp curls
Faintly outlined, vestigial laurel wreath,

Balanced between my forefinger and thumb,
My own the latest of a myriad hands
Infinitesimally to wear it smooth,

Reminds me: Rhegium, Reggio – I was there,
Had thumbed my way down from the Aspromont,
Dazed from its summits, springs, uncertain paths.

Dining alone, I watched across the café
Young Apollo, and marvelled at the sight
As I would not now (was I wrong then or now?).

I rub the coin, in profitless meditation,
To a new shine, burnishing an enigma
Too commonplace for words – at least my words.

On the reverse, Apollo's other visage:
Frontal, bristling, savage, a lion mask
Crowding the bronze with its terrific frown.

Exactly drawn, the little eyes and ears;
The lowering forehead and the whiskered jaws
Furrowed in high relief, proof against wear.

For this I have no matching memory,
But intimations enough: metamorphosis
Direly sudden as the flipping of a coin.

## ARDASHIR

### 1

Pitted and dulled, its copper showing through,
A Sassanid tetradrachm: Ardashir
Boils up, or seems to, from the silver alloy –

The absurd head-dress, elaborately unique
(Hardly to those for whom the coin was current
Any occasion for irony or a smile),

The filleted diadem, the braided beard,
The wedge-shaped eye with its indented pupil
Laying the regal face inscrutably open

For power to issue out, to scrutinise
Each rebel cranny of geography or mind,
A staring insight reaching through to the last

Recess of wilderness or crowded court
– So it had proved, so it was understood,
Ahriman prostrate under the trampling hoof.

On the reverse, as always, a fire-altar:
Difference of cult and place, of lore and myth
Cancelled in that unvarying conflagration,

An orthodoxy fierce as the heretic
It makes and burns; the image, standardised,
Retains its force (if by some freak of wear) –

Ravelling flames caught and intensified
By a desert wind, blown back upon themselves
But greedily rooting down and amply fed.

## 2

Were there to be no other motifs? The head-dress
Various indeed, radiate, turreted, winged
– Korymbos, crescent, star – through thirty types

Across one dynasty and four hundred years,
But the stare beneath the complicated crown
Set and direct as ever – if toward the end

Hollowed out, evasively desperate. I had seen
That stare, fixed by its mood, steady in its prime
On the basalt faces, heavily intent,

Of delicate-shawled Immortals carved in frieze
On the platform of the tumbled Apadana,
Soldiers of the lost Achaemenids on guard still

As Ardashir must have seen them. I had scrambled
Up a steep valley-side over tawny shale
To the castle-eyrie where an original strength

Had mustered once to restore the ancient rule;
Found my way through between the outer walls
Buttressed with pilasters, to a ruined hall

Where in arched niches above me fluted stucco
Clung to the rough-hewn stones, its pattern taken
(This too) from the lintels of sacked Persepolis,

An 'adventitious decoration', perhaps,
Thus copied; also a kind of proof, a detail
Intrinsic to the greater continuity.

## FOUR CITIES

### 1

The beauty of this coin of Croton
– Heracles reclining, cup in hand,
Cushioned by the lion-skin which falls

Loosely away around his body
(The city's founder, paused a moment) –
Is predicated on destruction:

Sybaris levelled, even its site
For centuries uncertain, under
The silt, flood upon flood, of Crathis.

Look, on the obverse, unassuaged still,
Hera from her Lacinian shrine
Stares out with enmity in her face!

### 2

'Tauriformis' – Horace's coinage
For Aufidus charging from the hills
Rain-swollen, carrying before it

Worked fields and orchards, livings and lives:
From the same die this coin of Gela,
Remnant of a brief hegemony.

Minted perhaps to pay a victor's
Bounty? A tyrant's headstrong likeness
Depicted beneath the curving horn?

Who knows? – the scarcely identified
Rubbish of obscure contingency
Swept clear now by the image, the word.


## 3

Here she is, the complacent goddess,
The Periclean triumphalist,
Her greedy, mirthless, archaic smile

Barely contained in the fat silver:
We suffer her still – the olive sprig
Pinned like a poppy ('Let England close'),

The puffed-up owl with its little beak,
Her alter ego, well pleased to peck
Random gobbets from learning's vitals…

Who dug the silver at Laurium?
What nameless suffering was the cost?
What is this virtue of mine that asks?

TARENTUM

Riding side-saddle on a dolphin
(Or shown in the act of dismounting?)
Taras arrives to found a city...

There, since no lodging was to be had,
I walked out beyond the last houses
And went to ground in open country,

My sleep walled by a stiff clay furrow;
Then back in the first of day, and down
To the foreshore of an inland sea

Where fishermen, returned, were sorting
Their catch and tackle: long-curled, clear-eyed,
Insouciant – as in the coin's time.

## ARETHUSA

Your braided hair a stream of water
Intact you hurry, a hidden spring
Past the circuit of plunging dolphins

To surface beside a distant shore
– Where I stood once, a secretive boy
With my parents, staring at a pool

Brackish with broken reeds, and failing
To match it to the myth. Your image,
Purely archaic, stamped in silver,

Reaches across the years, the passage
Of a lived life, to set me back there…
This time to find no contradiction.

## A COIN OF METAPONTUM

You look out at me from the silver
– The woman I am not equal to,
Your heavy hair mounded with harvest.

Had I known myself better in youth,
Had I trusted myself more fully,
I might have been your suitor. The years

Which have brought all that I could hope for
Have duly brought it late, too late now
Though I hold your coin, to need to hope

For you. But resting in your image,
The understanding of what I missed
Gifts me with a kind of possession.

## GALLO-ROMAN SUITE
*for M. -C.*

'Les Eaux et Forêts', Administration's phrase.

Incidentally beautiful, it evokes
Vistas, moments, journeys, but no clear picture.
The many glimpses crowd, one on another,
To make an indiscernible composite.

I look for a simile:
               the curving miles
Of poplar-skirted river, where no one reach
Or landing-place is separately recalled;
The dizzying sweep and sway, branch over branch,
Of shaken greenwood seen from its russet floor –
Images true in themselves.
                    But neither serves
For what, surprised, I discover in myself:
A loyalty, felt and not seen, requiring
Some talisman or token, not a likeness.

*

In place then of my similes, two objects.

Suddenly these have a meaning which for years
Eluded me as, puzzled, I handled them,
Asking why I still kept them, and impatient
Of vain accumulation – part of the weight,
Surely, of aging.
                Now they are freshly found:

The one, an awkward fragment of moulded tile,
Brick-red, grainy, picked from uneven rubble
Under sticks and leaves in a forest clearing
– The sanctuary once, a faded notice
Informed me, of the Gallo-Roman godhead,
Mercury;
        kept, since how could I throw away,
Without some sacrilege done to an obscure
Attachment, a relic of such provenance?


        *


The other, a coin:
        Postumus, the portrait
So lively he might be known at once, although
Next to nothing is known. By necessity
A usurper, he survived nine years, his brief
To hold the Rhine; was killed by his own soldiers
Shielding a frontier city from their pillage.

On the weakly struck reverse: a galley prow,
The word LAETITIA.
        A chip at the coin's edge
Shows its patina running right through the bronze,
Grey-green, muted – continuous with the shade,
Tracked by me, of an anciently diverted
Stream-bed, bounding the seat of the Gaballi
(Now melted into the village-name, Javols),

Where his milestone pillar was unearthed and stands.

## AFTER BASKERVILLE

Of typefaces in the nineteenth century
I read, 'Ingenuity replaces taste'.
And where had taste led, Baskerville's fonts
In the *Gazette Nationale*?
                                 Straight to the guillotine,
The clean cut of print to that of the blade.

## RICHTER

Awkward Atlas labouring under his gift
Until at the keyboard he could set it down

– A whimsical boyish sensitivity
Latent in his manner, lightening the trim
Heavy standoffish presence;
                              no uncalled-for
Movement at the piano, or afterwards
As he made his bow;
                        except, as if amused,
To pluck at the bouquet presented to him
For some strange flower, nicely superfluous.

This potsherd from the rim of a cup
Or jug – hardly a thing to be prized
In itself, a fragmentary fond
Keepsake from childhood – recalls the day,
Recalls the precise moment indeed,
When stumbling over fresh-furrowed ground
On that bare plateau I picked it up,
And brushing away some crumbs of earth,
Saw the patterned roundels underneath
– Six of them, delicately incised
(I thought, with the cut stem of a reed)
Before firing, in the still-wet clay.

An ancient cart-track had brought us out,
Past rock-hewn tombs, on a vague terrain
Impregnable walls had once secured:
There the lost city had pulsed with life,
Rome's equal, the blank alternative…
Was that the day when antiquity
– The place where all is over and done –
Took ineluctable hold of me?
How readily I had understood
An emptiness, mine to enter – yet
Where there was some object to retrieve,
A shape to counter the vacancy!

'Heu Veii veteres!', Propertius
Exclaimed. But the place is triply old
For me as I construe his verses:
Old already in the long-ago
That was his present, then for the child

Pleased with his find; old lastly for me
When I recollect that child, that day.
'Gone the throne of ivory and gold,
The battlements, the boundary-stones.
A shepherd's piping unwinds its slow
Improvised tune here. Uncaringly
Men reap their corn from among your bones.'

That moment of searching in the plough
While adults called me to 'come along',
Hurriedly choosing which sherd to keep
(My other finds were dispensable,
Since patternless): where does it belong?
Like Veii, to a history closed,
To a buried site? Or else not so,
If, the sherd between my fingers now,
Picked from the clutter it lay among,
Tokens, oddments, on my work-table,
I try out words for the broken shape,
The roundels regularly disposed?

## TOWARD KAYSERI

**1**

Jolted from somnolence I saw the mountain.
It filled the bus window, hanging in air
Immense and sudden, an anomalous wonder
Wholly out of scale with the threadbare patchwork
Of fields that lay beneath. Waking to it
Before I had fully woken to myself
I gazed in disbelief. It seemed to float
On vacancy, uncannily upheld –
A scarf of unseen mist across its base,
The slopes above hazed in sunshot vapour,
The summit silver-metalled with flashing snow
At once remote and overbearingly near
As the eye reached to it.
                              Then the bus turned,
We came down to a city, so to the next
Stage of a journey, the last stage soon lost
In the hurry of moving on – the journey also
Soon to be unremembered separately,

One in a palimpsest of youthful journeys.

**2**

Was that toward Kayseri?

                             Still after many years
The vision of the mountain kept returning.
Where and when had I seen it? Had I seen it?
My disbelieving wonder became a doubt –
Surely it must have been a waking dream,
Perhaps some local feature, nondescript,
Seen unawares, distortingly magnified?
Had the intimation of some larger land
Deluded me, the one that Youth imagines
On setting out, and hopes despite itself
To reach and know, an air-drawn shadow-ideal
Haunting the actual journey? A cloud-effect
Merely? The thing was too exceptional,
Could not be properly taken in, it bulked
Too large. And the memory remained adrift,
Nameless, too easily consigned by me
To the unverifiable…

           I chanced,
Looking through a sale catalogue one day,
On a photograph of Greco-Roman coins,
Provincial issues: a congeries of cities,
Of variant myth – nymph, hero, deity –,
Of vanished lore and cult.
           Among the lots
A group stood out which showed on the reverse
A little mountain, always the same motif
Crowding the field, a grandly present mass
(Crowned sometimes by a statue or a star)
Figured as if the die-cutters themselves
Had lived beneath… Image and memory
Suddenly crossed, filled me with recognition.
I checked the catalogue entry: 'Caesarea'.
Kayseri. It had indeed been on that road.
Here was the mountain I had glimpsed, and lost
Through my incuriousness, so long before:
'Mons Argaeus', placed at last and named,

What I'd thought irrecoverable reclaimed.

## MERTON STREET

### 1

The garden, how known!
                              the trampled grass,
the tree-peony, the climbing rose
which spread itself out against the wall
but hardly seemed to climb,
                              the fuchsia,
its arrowy blooms touched at the stub
with honey when split against the tongue,

the wistaria slowly thickening
from delicate slip to rigid coil,

the apricot tree, its bark incised
between swelling lips with a long scar
gnawed by a squirrel (so it was said),
the hardy luscious fruit, two or three
scant survivors reaching to ripeness
scarred themselves, divided among us
and eaten, as if that were plenty,

the exact spot where the first iris
flowered each year
                              – delphiniums, lupins,
snapdragons, lilies-of-the-valley,
each kind an absolute of design,

the wall of Oolitic limestone,
its flaking surface patched and calcined,
where tilted lintel and blocked window
were anciently immured,
                              and stunted
cypresses rooted amid crumbling
mortar, aloof from the raffish crowd
of wall-flowers or sterner London-pride,

the metal swing with a strip beneath
worn bare where heels rasped to a standstill
after soaring flight,
                              the makeshift hearth
where between sunken stones the kindled
fire burnt down to a nest of embers
and potatoes roasted in the ash,
their smouldering skins scraped softly out
– a white meat buttery and cindered
sweet and warm in the mouth,
                              the sandpit,
site of a Carthage half-built, half-dreamt,
tower, palace, castle, a summer's-worth
all raised and razed within two square yards
– width of the original ox-hide

for a foundation without deceit,
a destruction without consequence.

## 2

Unentered how many years the loft
above the carriage-house,

                            now garage,
there before us at the garden's end,
windowless, faded, powdery brick.

Below, all was explored, familiar:
workbench and tools, tincans and bottles,
a paraffin lamp, the car itself –
sleek household deity, stabled in
the blended mustiness.

                        Overhead,
a space unsanctioned, barely thought-of
or, if acknowledged, *Don't go up there,*
*the boards are rotten.* Worm-eaten stairs
had fractured and fallen in, a gap
too wide to jump.

                      The prohibition
lay mildly on me, as mere good sense.

Yet a desire to trust my lightness
to the rotten boards, to broach the space
nagged as if an equivalent space,
unbroached in my own head, were keeping
something from me

                      to be recovered,
and claimed as mine.

                      I found an entry
circuitously, as if by chance
one day, disobedient at last,
up a rusty fire-escape, along
a further wall, flat-topped, crawlable,

then through an opening at the side
where a warped clapboard had pulled away.

*

I stood and looked about me.
                              Nothing
was there but the dusty twilit space
– or nothing but my own presence there
unseen, suddenly out of the reach
of the life in common. 'There' was 'here',
and now I was wholly on my own –
no praise, no censure – what must follow?

I crossed to the middle of the floor
and sat, alert to the vacancy,
the silence, restless still,
                              and noticed
how at my feet some straw, discoloured,
had spilled from a rift beside a beam.

Aimlessly reaching in, I began
to pull away, by brittle handfuls,
what had sifted there,
                              until my grasp
did close on something. An excitement
filled me, belonging to the moment
which anticipates discovery,
knows that it is about to happen,
is happening…
                              Heavy in my hand
it lay, between my opened fingers,
a disc of brass, and at its centre
tarnished petals, a silver rosette.

I brushed and blew away the straw-dust,
examining it – a harness-piece
that had slipped down a century since
unmissed perhaps, unlooked-for, hidden
in its cranny,
                      to be fetched out now
into my day, the loft derelict,
the horses gone.
                      I rummaged further
but found nothing. My find had been made.


                      *


I crawled out into sunlight, along
the wall,
                down the rusty fire-escape
back to the garden, the trampled lawn
and, as I crawled, could feel the horse-brass
weighing in my pocket,
                            a trophy
which, after polishing, I would add
to my collection of rarities

– coin, fossil, crystal, mineral, sherd –

so that, reclaimed, it might have its place
and shine, as the fact of meaning should.

## THE LOFT

I tease the memory for what it might mean:
In that bare loft nothing was to be seen –
Nothing, or was there something after all?
Some detail, overlooked and incidental,
Or made light of, so light that it need not
Be mentioned, a triviality – and yet
Heavy in the finding, a name, a fact
Largely substantial, describable, exact.

## ACKNOWLEDGEMENTS AND NOTES

Many of these poems were included in a pamphlet, *A Last Look* (Mica Press, 2016). 'The Coin Cabinet' first appeared in *The Rialto*, 'Ionian' in *Agenda*, and 'Loggerhead' in the *Times Literary Supplement*. Two poems from my *Collected Poems* (Carcanet, 2009) are reprinted here, 'By the Loire' to make an addition, 'The Alfred Jewel' to make a correction.

My special thanks to Leslie Bell of Mica Press, also to Benoit Wells and to Justine Gomes.

\*

'The Coin Cabinet': I love Greek coins and cannot afford to collect them, or hardly so. This is my virtual collection. My subject is the way in which the coins of each city (there are a myriad cities) sum up a particular place and the life of a place in a chosen image, an instance of concentrated design. Put together, the many images represent the variousness of a world – that world from which, at the close of the fourth stanza, Hermes escorts the recent dead, and to which Persephone returns at the close of the fifth. It is my fancy that the exact syllable-count stands for the exactness of the stamped design, while the irregular rhythms stand for the coins' irregularities of shape.

For some information and phrasing I am indebted to G.K. Jenkins, *Ancient Greek Coins* (Barrie & Jenkins, 1972).

'Loggerhead': I was thinking of seventeenth-century emblem poems. But the turtle is a real one, seen off the island of Melos some forty years ago. A turtle also figures on the coins of Aegina, the earliest to be minted in Europe.

'Monte Gennaro Revisited': The 'Campanile' is the name locally given to the cliff-escarpment of an outlying spur of Monte Gennaro.

'From an Old Notebook': The syntax in lines two and three of *Hand touches hand...* ' is elliptical. 'touches' in line three is a verb (as it is in the other lines), governed here by the subject noun 'branch' in line two. 'But' = 'only has to'.

'The Fall of Winston': The line-breaks are meant to be of the very slightest weight, a subliminal punctuation pacing the narrative. Since free verse is so dependent upon enjambment, as the one principal technique of formal verse to be retained, I think our contemporary ear tends to hear it too emphatically, rather as metrical verse was heard too emphatically in the later nineteenth century.

'Group with Laptop': The painting is the one at Chatsworth, not Poussin's later treatment of the 'Et in Arcadia Ego' theme in the Louvre.

'The Alfred Jewel': The Jewel (in the Ashmolean) terminates in a gold boar's head. So read 'beast-mouth' as here, not 'wolf-mouth' as I misremembered when the poem first appeared. The poem commemorates a friend, Max Anderson, who was ambushed by mental illness and died young in unclear circumstances. There was indeed a beast about.

'At Kirtlington': The quarry at Kirtlington, near Oxford, has now been made into a park with fenced-off walkways. In those days it was deserted and its rich fossil beds lay open. Lamellibranch and brachiopod are two kinds of bivalve mollusc, the halves of the shell of the lamellibranch meeting evenly at the hinge, while in the brachiopod one half comes to a point which reaches over the other. The *ch* in both words is hard.

'Near Charnizay': A hamlet in the southern Touraine.

'Ardashir': Ardashir founded the Sassanid dynasty which

defeated and replaced the Parthians as rulers of Persia, to be defeated and replaced in turn after some four hundred years, following the Moslem Arab invasion of Persia in the mid-seventh century. The Sassanians (the name derives from Sasan, said to be the father of Ardashir) saw themselves as heirs of the Achaemenids (Cyrus, Darius, Xerxes, and their successors) and revivers of the ancient Persian empire founded by Cyrus. Persepolis was the capital of the Achaemenid heartland (also the Sassanian heartland) in what is now the province of Fars in south-west Iran. It was put to the sack by Alexander and the royal palace left in ruins. The 'apadana' is the pillared audience-hall of the palace.

Sassanian kings went in for elaborate headdresses. Each king had his own version and can be recognised by it on his coins. The 'korymbos' was a large globe of stuffed cloth which often topped the headdress. Ardashir's 'castle-eyrie', from which he staged his revolt against the Parthians, lies across a steep-sided gorge near Firuzabad. The Sassanians also went in for immense propagandising rock-carved friezes, one of which shows Ahriman, the Devil of Zoroastrian belief, trampled under the horse of Shapur, Ardashir's son and successor. Zoroastrianism was the enforced state religion.

For some information and phrasing I am indebted to Roman Ghirshman, *Iran: Parthians and Sassanians*, translated by Stuart Gilbert and James Emmons (Thames and Hudson, 1962).

'Four Cities' (1): Croton and Sybaris were rival Greek cities lying (like Metapontum) between the heel and toe of Italy. In 510 B.C. Sybaris, a byword for wealth and luxury, was obliterated by Croton. Heracles was said to have founded Croton while stopping there to rest on the way back from his tenth Labour (the oxen of Geryon). The Lacinian shrine, its ruins still to be seen, lay on a promontory just outside Croton.

(2): Aufidus, in Apulia, was Horace's native river, compared in *Odes* 4.14, when in spate, to a bull and to a conquering general on the battlefield, the poem commemorating the conquest. Gela was briefly in the early fifth century B.C. the dominant Greek city in Sicily. Its coins show a river-god in the shape of the forepart of a charging bull, but with a man's features.

(3): Coins of Athens in the mid-fifth century heyday of its imperial pretensions unvaryingly show the head of Athena, and on the reverse her totem owl and an olive sprig. The silver came from mines at Laurium in Attica. The cited phrase, pointing the contemporary reference, is from Ted Hughes's 'Remembrance Day', the third part of his poem 'Out'.

'Tarentum': Tarentine coins show, with many variants of which this is one, the city's mythical founder, Taras, son of Poseidon, arriving on a dolphin. The city was built on an isthmus which partly encloses a large sea-inlet.

'Arethusa': Arethusa tells her story in Ovid's *Metamorphoses*, Book 5, and in Thom Gunn's imitation, 'Arethusa Saved', in *Boss Cupid*. Her spring surfaces beside the harbour of Syracuse. Coins of the city show her head surrounded by dolphins.

'A Coin of Metapontum': The woman figured on some coins of Metapontum is Demeter, the goddess who represents 'the life of fruits and corn'.

'Gallo-Roman Suite': 'L'Administration des Eaux et Forêts' is the name, anciently given, of the government department which has charge of France's state-owned woods and waterways. The chief Gallic deity was identified with the Roman Mercury and assumed his name (while he also kept his local names). Postumus, in effect first king of France *avant la lettre*, ruled from 259 to 268 A.D. The 'frontier city' was Mayence (Mainz). The 'seat of the Gaballi' was the town of Anderitum, now farms and fields at the head of a shallow valley in the southern Massif Central. The 'milestone pillar', its elegantly lettered inscription naming Postumus, is the centrepiece of the little museum in Javols, the village at the edge of the site.

'After Baskerville': 'Baskerville's fonts were used to print the *Gazette Nationale, ou Le Moniteur Universel*, the official journal of the French Republic during "the terrible years".' D.B. Updike, *Printing Types* (Cambridge U.P., 1937).

'Richter': He was playing Schumann's Piano Quintet with The Borodin Quartet. This was in June 1994 at La Grange de Meslay, the tithe barn outside Tours where he founded a music festival. It was one of his last concerts.

'Veii': Veii, nine miles north across the Tiber, was Rome's early rival, the first of the cities that 'must be destroyed'. The site was afterwards abandoned.

'Toward Kayseri': Had I trusted my memory, the mountain which I came to think I had in some way imagined or exaggerated would have been easily identified. A vast extinct volcano, now called Mount Erciyes, it dominates the central Anatolian plateau near Kayseri. Mons Argaeus means 'the white mountain', Argaeus being cognate with 'argentum', and the image on the silver coins of Caesarea, where the mountain was the object of a cult, perhaps suggesting a play on words.

'Merton Street' (1): The legend goes that a piece of land no larger than might be covered by the hide of an ox was promised to the refugee Dido and her Phoenician followers. But the hide was then cut into a long fine strip, to surround and claim the hill of Bursa (an 'ox hide'), which became the citadel of Carthage and the site of the city's foundation.